Learning Tree
1 2 3

Shape

By Richard and Nicky Hales
Illustrated by Rebecca Archer

CHERRYTREE BOOKS

As you read this book, try to answer the questions and think of some questions of your own. Write your answers on a piece of paper or in a notebook – not in the book.
There are answers at the end of the book. Try not to look at them before you have had a try. If you find the questions too hard, ask a grown-up or older friend to help you.

A Cherrytree Book

Designed and produced by
A S Publishing

First published 1991
by Cherrytree Press Ltd
a subsidiary of
The Chivers Company Ltd
Windsor Bridge Road
Bath, Avon BA2 3AX

Copyright © Cherrytree Press Ltd 1991

British Library Cataloguing in Publication Data
Hales, Richard *1953-*
  Shape.
  1. Shape
  I. Title II. Hales, Nicky III. Archer, Rebecca IV. Series
  516

  ISBN 0-7451-5143-4

Printed and bound in Italy by L.E.G.O. s.p.a., Vicenza

All rights reserved. No part of this publication may be reproduced, stored in a retrieval system, or transmitted, in any form, or by any means without the prior permission in writing of the publisher, nor be otherwise circulated in any form of binding or cover other than that in which it is published and without a similar condition including this condition being imposed on the subsequent purchaser.

Folding shapes

You need three square pieces of paper.

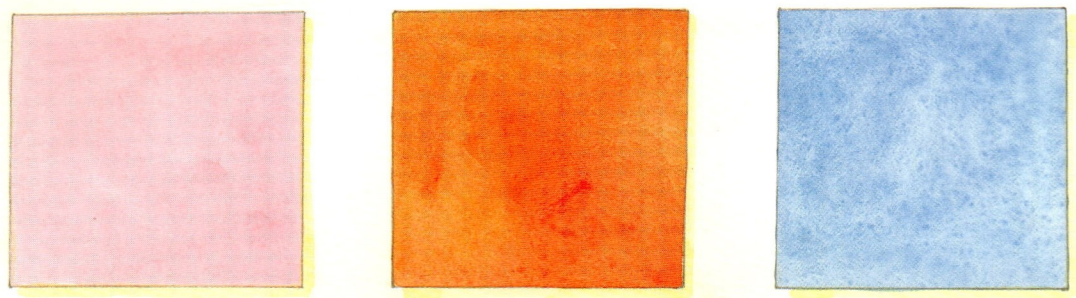

Can you fold one square to make two oblongs?

Can you fold another square to make two triangles?

How many folds to make 2 triangles?

Can you fold another square to make four squares?

How many folds to make 4 squares?

Squares

You need some short straws.

Make a square with four straws.

Make a bigger square with more straws.

Are all the squares the same size?

How many straws did you use?
How many squares have you made?

How many straws do you need to make this square?

How many squares have you made now?

How many large ones?

How many small ones?

Triangles

Use three straws to make a triangle.

Add more straws to make a bigger triangle.

How many straws did you use?
How many triangles have you made?
Are they all the same size?

Add more straws to make this triangle.

How many straws did you use?
How many triangles have you made?
How many large ones?
How many small ones?

Boxes and tins

Collect some containers from your kitchen.

Sort out the shapes with square faces.
Sort out the shapes with oblong faces.
Sort out the shapes with round faces.

Are there any containers that belong in more than one group?

Choose one of the containers.
Draw round one of its faces on a piece of paper.
Draw it again and again to make a pattern.
Make sure the faces touch each other.

Five-piece tangram

Fold a square piece of paper like this and then like this.

Colour some of the folds to make this picture.

Cut along the coloured lines.

What pictures can you make by putting the pieces of your tangram together?

Use some or all of the pieces.

Look at the pieces of your tangram.

How many large triangles are there?
How many small triangles?
How many squares?

Can you make a square with some or all of the pieces of your tangram?

Can you make a large triangle?
Can you make an oblong?

Can you make a house?
Can you make a boat?

Right angles

Find a scrap of paper.
Any shape will do.
Fold it in two.

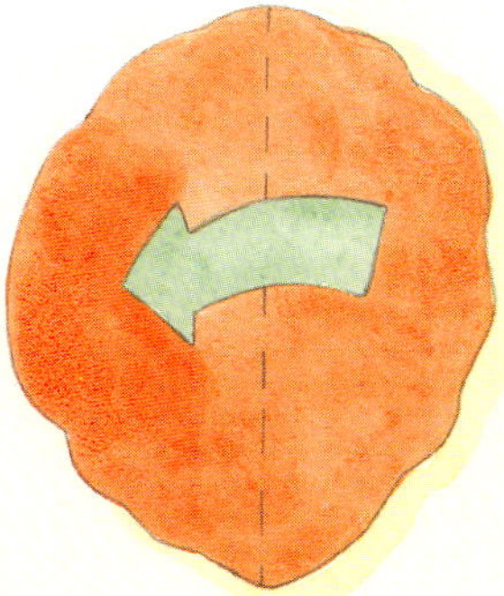

Fold it again keeping the straight edge in line.

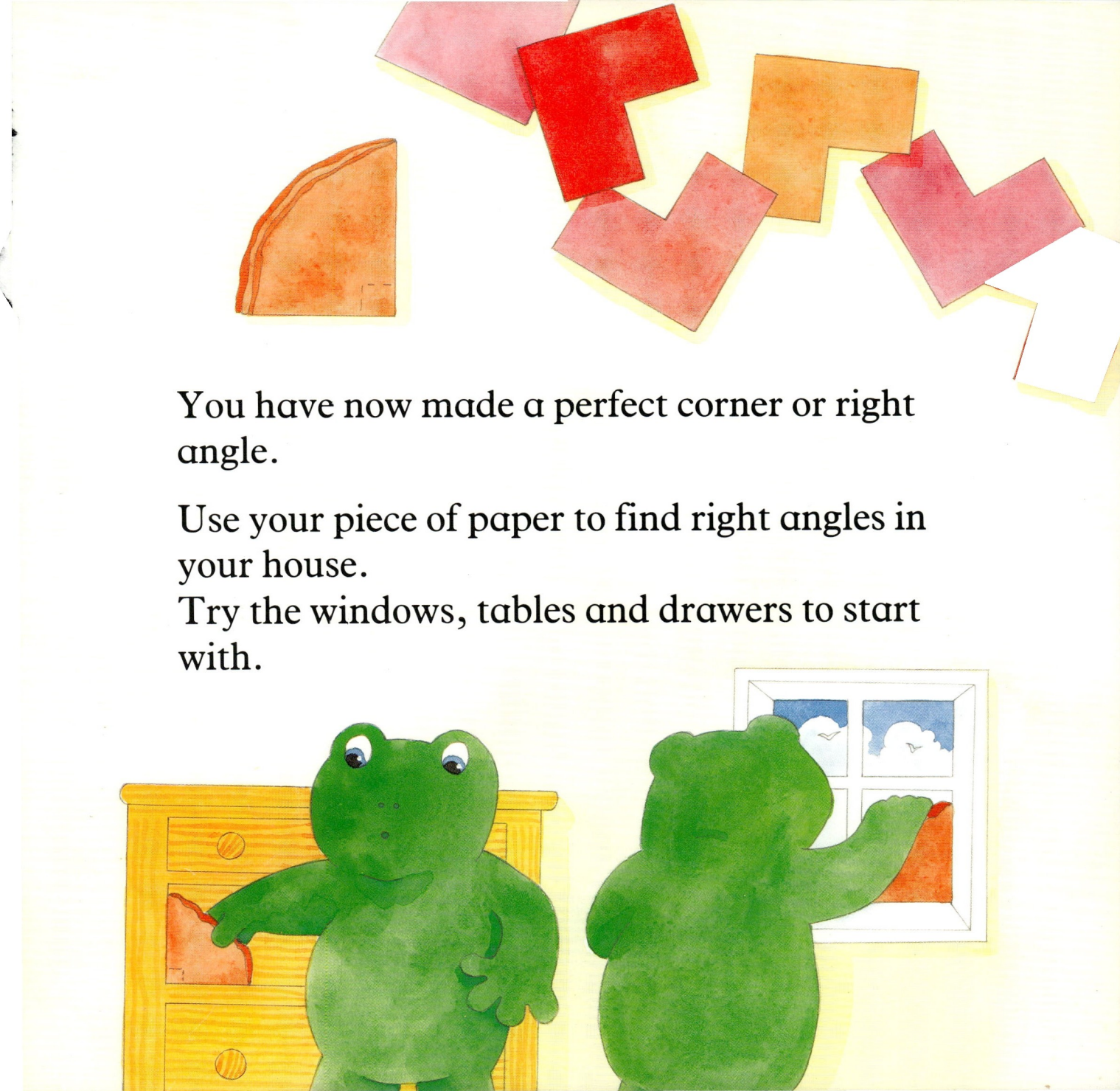

You have now made a perfect corner or right angle.

Use your piece of paper to find right angles in your house.
Try the windows, tables and drawers to start with.

Oblongs

You need some oblong domino shapes.
You can use real dominoes or make your own.
They need to be twice as long as they are wide.

How many different patterns can you make with four dominoes?

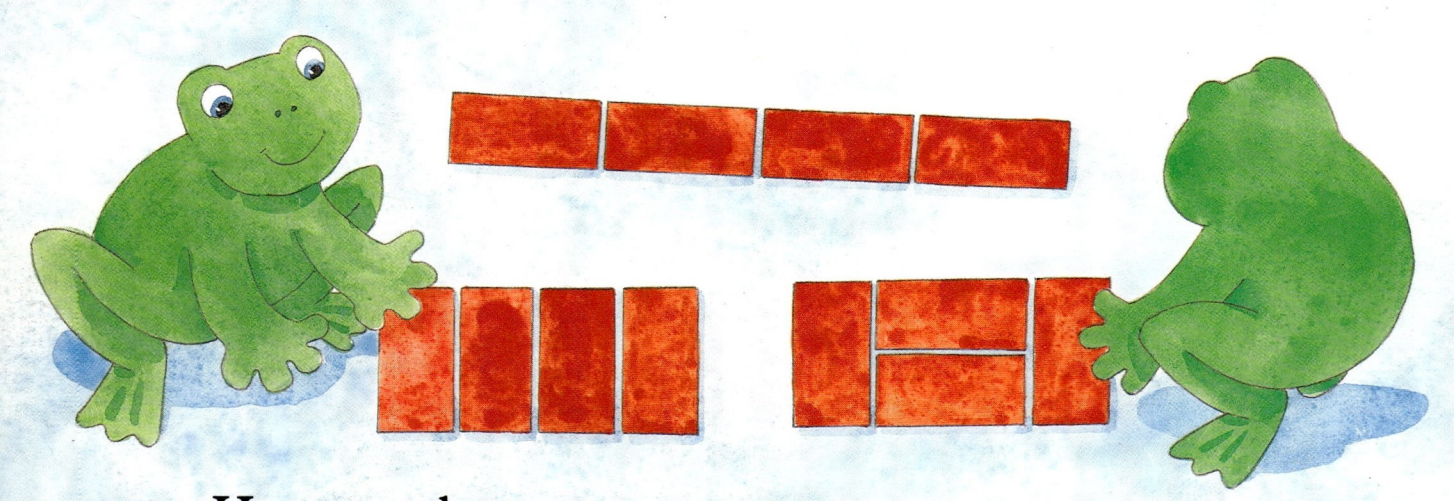

Here are three patterns.
How many more can you make?

How many patterns can you make with six dominoes?
Here is one pattern.

Domino squares

Put two dominoes together to make a square.

Can you make a square with eight dominoes?

How many ways can you put the dominoes together to make your square?
Draw a picture of each way.

More things to do

Make some shapes
Cut out some triangles, circles, squares and oblongs from coloured paper. Fit them together to make interesting patterns and pictures. Try using different sizes of the same shape, or squares and oblongs together. Draw pictures and patterns. Put a frame round your pictures, using coloured patterns.

Look for shapes
Look around your house and find squares and oblongs and circles. Are there many triangular things?

Look at things in the garden. What shapes are the leaves and trees? Draw a pattern of leaves.

Look at walls and buildings in the street. See the patterns the windows make. Draw a block of flats using oblongs and squares for the walls, doors and windows.

Look at your food. What shape are your sandwiches? What shape are your favourite sweets?

Writing
Look at the shapes you make when you write. Which letters have curves? Which ones have straight lines? Which ones have both?

Domino pictures
See what shapes or pictures you can make by joining 4 dominoes. Make your own domino shapes from coloured paper or draw the shapes.

Can you stack cans?
Look at the cans, cartons and packets in the supermarket. How are they stacked? Borrow some cans from the kitchen (ask first) and see how many ways you can stack them. Draw each way. Here are two ways of stacking six cans. How many more can you find?

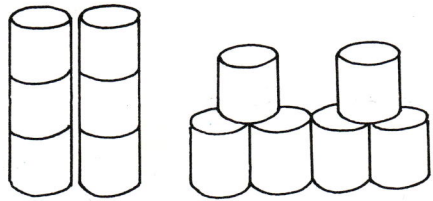

1

1 What shape is the sun?

2 What shape is this book?

3 Can you fold a square piece of paper to make four triangles? How many folds did you need?

4 How many straws do you need to make a square?

5 What shapes can you see in this picture?

2

6 What shape is the moon? Is it always the same shape?

7 What things do you play with that are twice as long as they are wide?

8 What shape is a newspaper?

9 Which is the odd one out: sphere, ball, cube, globe? Why?

10 How many dominoes do you need to make a letter H? What about a T, U or an S?

11 Choose a small carton or container. Draw round it over and over to make a pattern that has no gaps.

12 How many right-angles are there on the cover of this book?

13 Can you fold a square piece of paper to make four oblongs? How many folds do you have to make?

3

14 Using the pieces of the five-piece tangram on page 10, can you find other ways to make squares, triangles and oblongs?

15 Can you fold a square piece of paper to make an envelope? How many folds do you need? What shapes do you end up with?

16 How many oblong patterns can you make with eight dominoes?

17 Look at solid objects. Find out what these shapes look like: a cube, a cone, a cylinder, a pyramid, a sphere.

18 Can you make this square with a hole in the middle with four dominoes? Can you make it with twelve?

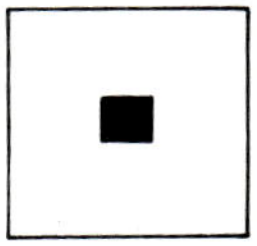

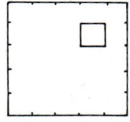

19 Can you make a 12-domino square and leave the hole here?

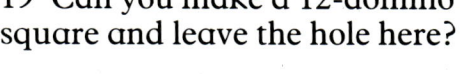

20 Find out what the word *tesselate* means.

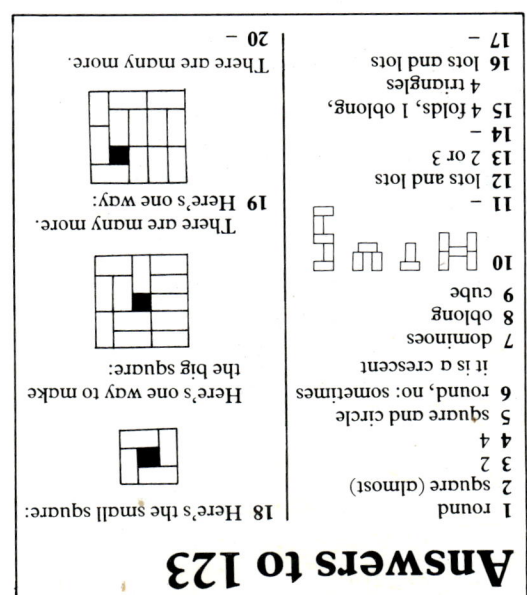

Answers to 123

1 round
2 square (almost)
3 2
4 4
5 square and circle
6 round, no; sometimes it is a crescent
7 dominoes
8 oblong
9 cube
10
11 –
12 lots and lots
13 2 or 3
14 –
15 4 folds, 1 oblong, 4 triangles
16 lots and lots
17 –
18 Here's the small square:
19 Here's one way:
There are many more.
Here's one way to make the big square:
There are many more.
20 –

Index

boat 15
boxes and tins 10
cans 21
can you stack cans? 21
circles 3, 21
containers 10, 11
corner 17
dominoes 18-21
five-piece tangram 12
folding 4, 5, 12, 16

frame 21
house 15
look for shapes 21
make some shapes 21
oblong faces 10
oblongs 3, 4, 10, 15, 18, 21
patterns 11, 18, 19, 21
pictures 13, 21
right angles 16, 17
round faces 10

square faces 10
squares 3-7, 10, 12, 14, 15, 20, 21
straws 6-9
tangram 12-15
triangles 3, 5, 8, 9, 14, 15, 21
writing 21

Answers

Page 4
1 fold

Page 5
1 fold
2 folds

Page 6
12 straws
5 squares (4 small, 1 large)

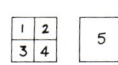

Page 7
24 straws
14 squares (9 small, 1 large, 4 medium)

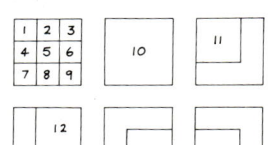

Page 8
9 straws
5 triangles (4 small, 1 large)

Page 9
18 straws
13 triangles (9 small, 1 large, 3 medium)

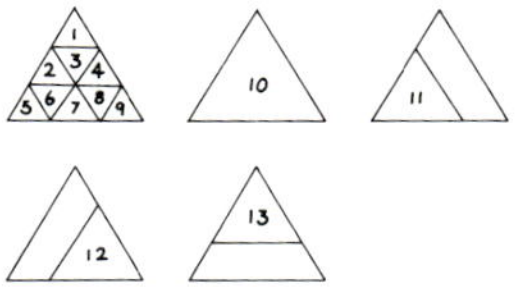

Page 14
2 large triangles
2 small triangles
1 square

Page 15
Here are some squares, triangles and oblongs

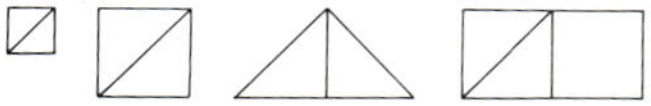

Here are a house and a boat:

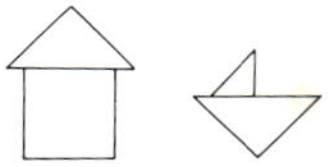

Page 18
Here are two 4-domino patterns:

Page 19
Here are six 6-domino patterns:

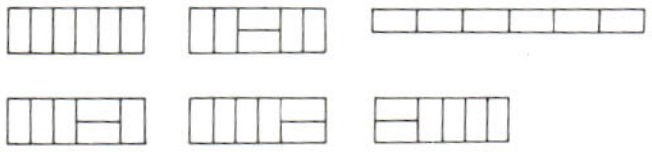

Page 20
Here are five 8-domino squares:

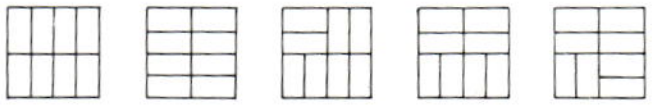